GW00702038

VISIONS

of

NORFOLK

a celebration
in free verse
by
Meryl Hirons

First Published in 1996 by
Monteney Community Workshop

Copyright © 1996 Meryl Hirons

All rights reserved. No parts of this publication may be
reproduced, stored in a retrieval system or transmitted in
any form or by any means of electronic, mechanical, photo
copying, recording or otherwise, without the prior permission
of the publisher and copyright holder.

ISBN 1 872934 36 6

**Monteney Community Workshop
Sheffield England**

CONTENTS

VISIONS OF NORFOLK

There are so many days,
Busy and fraught
With problems end to end,
When, should you ask me,
I could not say with any certainty
Whether the sun had shone,
Or it had rained.

Later, in precious moments of repose,
Before sleep finally takes over
From my too-active brain,
My memory plays back
On eyelids' screen
My favourite visions,
Calming, nourishing ...

I see again an unfrequented stretch
Of Norfolk sands,
Unhurrying clouds,
The constant waves;
Imagine I feel the light winds fan
As I pick up cool stones
And sculptured shells -
Compare their colours, forms,
Discard some, selecting others,
Fill first my hands and then my pockets
With their multiple variety;
Wander far without realising,
Pass time peacefully.

Or I can conjure views
Of estuary and countryside,
Small villages of flint-built cottages,
Pink, white with blossom,
Basking in the sun;
Or huddled close, their ancient walls
Proof against winter's worst;
Churches, strung point-to-point
Across the fields;
The birds which gather, feed and fly,
Their daily rituals marked
By their distinctive calls.

I recollect the grandeur
Of the skyscape in a storm
And then the peace at evening tide
When sunset spreads
Its glories in the sky:
Rose, peach, primrose, apple,
Violet-stained.

It's then I recognise
My deep involvement with this place
To which I look forward
With an aching need
To the next time I can visit -
And the next -
Until I become one with it,
And I sleep at last ...

GLASSBLOWER AT WORK

We enter the viewing area:
The heat strikes out - it is too near,
Too much to bear. We stand back,
Ignore the proffered chairs.

Free of hampering cloth,
His muscles hard and lean
Rippling beneath a spotless T-shirt,
The glassblower works.

Rhythmically he moves from fire to bench,
From bench to fire,
Rolling, ever moving the metal bar,
Watchful and expert in his progress;

The gypsy-dark eyes intent
On the globule of molten glass
Drooping from the metal tube
He turns and turns again.

The sweat-band on his forehead, from which
A forelock has escaped to get a better view,
Restrains his long, dark hair,
The sweat beads queuing to fall.

At last, a deft knock with his shears:
Another item joins those for the kiln
To metamorphose colours, and emerge
A finished product for the shop.

CLEY MARSHES - EARLY SPRING

Wind siffles, rippling
The sea of grasses,
Reeds, which stand
Straight against the solemn sky.

A solo mallard flaps inland,
Its wing-beat sounding
In the still air
Like tissue paper, fidgeted.

Some martins dive and swoop -
First black, then invisible
As they turn against the gloom,
Then black again,
Chasing and turning
In generous circles,
But screaming desultorily as yet,
Knowing their season
Has not fully come.

Behind me in the pinewoods
Pigeons clap,
Make comfortable noises,
Settling for the night.

Streamers of blue-grey clouds
Stand still, set in pearly opalescence.
Dusk falls, subtly
Draining colour from the marsh -
Prepares it for the greater dark of night.

EVENING AT MARTHAM STAITHE

We came late in the day
To see if we could hire
A boat to tour the waterways
Next day; there were none -
But a kind boat-owner,
Seeing disappointment
In the children's eyes
Asked : 'Can you row?'
Offered his dinghy
For a half-hour trip.
And so we started out
As dusk was taking over
From the day.
He waved us off.

It took a little while
To recall the long-neglected skill
As we took the turning
Of the river's bend
Which hid the staithe from view.
But then the natural rhythm
Of the plash of oars,
The groan of rowlocks
Stilled even the excited
Children's chatter.

Then we came
Into a different world
Inches only from
The water's sheen,
The reed beds high
On either side.
We shipped our dripping oars,
Drifted with the stream;

Pointed silently to show
Each other what we saw :
A water-rat swam strongly
For the bank, its wake
A silvery vee behind it ;
A moor-hen's straggly nest,
Precarious, amongst the reeds;
And further on
The proud mound of a swan's
Superior dwelling,
A pair of swans atop, vigilant.
There were strange murmurs -
Little sounds,
Muted by proximity -
Not understood,
And yet somehow
Not needing explanation.

At last, a few late ducks flew down,
Descending to the water
With a whirr of wings,
Then aquaplaning on
The bubbling slip-stream
They had caused,
Making commotion
Which aroused
An echoing, sleepy protest
From some other bird.

The last glow from the sky
Lit eerily some wisps of mist
Which hung a little above
The surface of the water here,
And we knew , reluctantly,
We should, we must turn back.

LIFEBOAT

The maroon went at seven
That gloomy Spring morning -
Three immense thuds
Reverberating round.
Dream-troubled,
Sleep-shattered,
I struggled to liveliness,
Guessed, somehow knew,
What that sound must mean.

I pulled on warm clothes,
Left the door on the latch,
Fled to the cliff-top
To spy over the bay;
Saw the curved wake
Carved in cold, heaving grey
As the lifeboat left shelter
And headed to sea.

Seen as so sturdy,
Filling the boathouse,
On show to tourists
In off-duty hours,
Now in the context
Of high-lashing waters
It's merely another
Frail craft out there -

Pitching and yawing,
Staggering to progress,
Only its wheelhouse
Is to be seen -
Its garish fluorescence
The watcher's reassurance,
Alternate with white spume
Flung by the waves.

What of the men on board?
All sons and fathers
Of local families
Well-known in the town.
They know the dangers,
Cannot explain to you
Why they race to take risks
As great as these are -
Except to say, simply,
When pressed for an answer:
"It's something we've always done,
It's in the blood".

They're caring for seafarers -
Brothers or strangers -
In the way that they know best,
Pitting deep knowledge
Of their own local waters
Against fickle elements'
Capricious whim;
Their modest claim
When a rescue's effected:
Keeping up a proud record,
Their job's been well done.

BLAKENEY - APRIL EVENING

We walk along the bank
Where clumps of coarse grass
Toss, buffeted, at our feet.

We hear a mysterious sound,
Like alpine goats' bells,
Discordant, sweet,
Both distant, near at hand -
Puzzle, then find
Above tarpaulined bodies
Of the boats beached high,
Thin metal rigging beats
On thin metal masts;
Playing vibrato, pizzicato,
Syncopated rhythms
Orchestrated by the wind
Which whistles through
Half-closed lips,
Encouraging its musicians
To an unknown score;
Pennants in the gods applaud.

Now, to the West,
The ebb-tide runs
Along the channels to the sea:
The ooze it leaves
Shines silver in the light
And estuarial waders
Probe out their evening meal.

Dusk softens detail :
The land lies dreaming
All along to Cley -
Ponds, reeds, meadows, fields -
The distant hillocks crowned
With greening trees of Spring.

The air is filled with lark-song
And the sudden cry
Of sea birds as they pass.
Coots start a water -battle
Which nesting ducks observe.
A hawk hovers, plummets;
There's a brushing of the air
As an owl glides by.

Soon, shadowy clouds
Will close the shutters
Of the sky, allowing
The reddened eye of day
One final glimpse
Before it sinks to rest.

COLD DAY ON THE COAST

Grey sky, grey sea..
The sullen slap
Of waves on shore:
Grey shingle shifts forward,
Rattles back ...
Even horizon wears a grey mist veil.

A fitful breeze,
Devoid of power -
Or sun to give it warmth -
Winnows disinterestedly
The silvery grains
Of sand, heaped
Where the marram grass
Breaks through.

A grey-backed gull
Glides, silent, by -
Wheels,
Sweeps past again, and I,
Hands clenched in pockets,
Hunch deeper in my coat -
Stride out towards home.

WEYBOURNE STATION - LOW SEASON

The scent of conifers greets us
As we turn in
Before the station buildings.
We park beside the huge old water tank
Near to the soot-scarred bridge.

Our feet crunch gravel as we walk,
Pass through the rustic gate
To gain the deserted platform.
Sounds of industry waft
From the workshops along the line:
The volunteer band is present even now -
We know, accept their dedication.

Wild poppies shake with the breeze,
Their wiry stems triumphing
Through stone chippings
To bring their heads to birth
Beside the track.

Great sheeted hulks
Of former giants of steam
Stand mutely in the salty winds
Which cut across the cornfields
From the sea;
While in the expansive canvas
Of pale sky,
Gulls make their wheedling cries
And Weybourne Mill stands sentinel.

AFTERNOON IN AYLSHAM

Into the church-yard now.
Through the shady lych -
Over the cattle-grid
Thoughtfully placed
Long years ago
To keep stray animals out
On market days
Should drovers fail
To keep control of beasts
They'd bought,
Or brought for sale.

The clock in the tall, square
Tower of stone and flint,
Emits a welcoming, mellow chime
('Westminster'- no less!)
Above, the golden cockerel faces
Steadfastly south-east,
Glows in the April sun
Against the brilliant, breezy blue.

Somewhere a pheasant crucks
Its warning note;
Chaffinches see-saw
In the ragged yews
Which line the boundary
Of the church's grounds.

The low brick wall
Which marks the rising path
Is topped with lichens
Prospering in the light.
Clumps of wild flowers,
Clustered on the lawns, comfort
The mourning stones of graves,
Give interest to the orange-bottomed bees
Busying themselves in sonorous flight;
A tortoiseshell flutters past
Settles to sip nectar, flutters on ...

This is a place to sit
And contemplate eternal truths -
Or bask, and think of nothing,
In the warmth.

SCOLT HEAD TRIP

It's fine June weather.
We arrive at the Staithe
In time to find 'The Sea Pearl'
Making ready to cast off
For Scolt Head Island, over there;
We will not miss this chance.

Once on board, we soon get underway.
The breeze is fresh,
Wafting the stink of diesel
From the housing where
The drubbing engine
Reverberates,
Rattling our teeth
As the prow rises to crest
Cross-waves, meeting us.

Yachts ride at anchor,
Rock to our swell;
My camera frames
An impression, Monet-esque:
'Sailing Boats at Brancaster'.
We pass them by,
Soon see our landing point.

We crunch over shingle,
Buy a guide book,
Follow the Nature Trail;
Sun warms us as we start.
The air is filled
With the constant scream
Of ground-nesting birds;
You need binoculars,
They're so well camouflaged.

We keep to the marked path,
Look out for Sea-holly,
Bird's-foot-trefoil,
White sea campion, Thrift ...
Shade our eyes against
The brilliant sky,
Delighting in a lark
Which bubbles overhead;
See periwinkle - blue
And copper butterflies flit
From bush to flower, on, on,
Always a little way ahead.

We stop at point 6
To eat our sandwiches, just by
The spiky marram grass of dunes:
Look one way to the land
The other to shore -
Then watch, fascinated,
A Little Tern fly, hover,
Fold wings, plunge to fish
Beneath the surface of the waves.

It's time to go!
We start back for the boat,
Gathering souvenirs:
A shell, a whelk's egg-case,
A sun-bleached stick ...

Later, the engine-note alters,
Slowing as we come to shore,
Grate into shallow water.
Money changes hands,
We walk the plank,
Helped by the cheery boatman;
The trip is over,
But not in our heads.

HEACHAM LAVENDER - JULY

We first smelt the fields
From several miles away,
Suddenly on the summer-laden air:
Soft, sensuous, sweet,
Head-high, lung-deep
The perfume met us.

"Where are they?", "Can we see?"
But while all around us lie
Ordinary fields of yellow, green and gold,
There are none of royal purple
Such as we thought to find.

We come to Caley Mill
And see laid out
The National Collection -
Neat rows of every shade
Of lavender from blue
Through mauve to pink,
All labelled to denote their pedigree.

We watch the men at work
In the distillery,
Forking to the boilers' mouths
Cropped lavender, still busy with bees
Clinging inebriate to the clumps,
Drinking the sweetness till the last.
We hear how much of this beauty
Is strained to make a little phial.

We have cream teas, visit the shop
And buy things to remind us.
As we leave, tractors still trundle,
Carrying in their scented burdens
From fields we never found.

THORNHAM CREEK

You approach the distant
Mauve-blue line which is the sea
Down long, straight lanes
Between high, limey clumps
Of some umbellifer in bud;
You go on till,
Quite suddenly,
The lane becomes a path,
Lined on each side
By flaxen reeds
Bent to the tune of winds
Beside the estuary.

You come, eventually,
To a point where channels meet.
Sit, for a time,
Sun warm on your back;
Hear gulls skirl, larks burble,
Bees zoom,
See boats moored, tilted at angles,
High and dry above the sage-brown mud.

Gauge by the tonsured banks
The depth of water
Which flow-tide will bring
And while away the intervening time
By watching the sun
Play racing games with billowy clouds -
Green-brown across the heath,
Touching the sea to silver,
Lighting the dunes to gold.

THE THURSFORD EXPERIENCE

Crashy and clashy,
Garish and glorious,
Colours, sounds, lights
All flashy and loud -
When one organ's finished
Then up starts another:
We watch in delight
As they pound out their tunes.

The bright painted figures,
Mechanically moving,
Conduct, play an instrument,
Strike cymbals or bells;
There's all kinds of music,
From marches to dances -
We find it nostalgic,
Exciting and rare.

The children are loving
Each roistering moment,
It's impossible
To **not** get a lift out of this !
All around, people
Are smiling and nodding,
Are swaying and tapping
To rhythm and beat.

At last, having heard
These magnificent instruments,
There are steam traction engines
To see and admire,
And time for a ride
On the Venetian Gondolas,
Elaborate, gold-painted,
Exotic and plush.

We sit down to enjoy
The Wurlitzer Concert -
Spectacular playing
Of tunes new and old -
The organist's famous
For pleasing his audience -
Treats us to his programme
With flair and panache.

A great afternoon !
We agree as we leave now,
A time we'll remember
For a long while ahead;
And when we visit Norfolk
Next year on our holidays,
We promise ourselves,
That this place is a must.

THE WEAVERS OF WORSTEAD

Six centuries old, St. Mary's Church,
Handsome in flint, its sturdy form complete,
Regarding with maternal care
The small community it's overseen
Through times of fame, decline,
Is now home to a Guild
Which Spinners and Weavers formed
To revive the dying craft.

Now weavers travel rural miles to meet,
Preside on summer evenings in the aisles
Working their looms, their spinning wheels,
Chatting with whoever will call in;
Proud to show the products of their hands:
Pew-runners, kneelers, curtains, altar cloths...

Colours blend, tremble, come alive,
Step out from warp and weft
As with sure strokes the weavers work
Their patterns, yield another length of cloth -
Humbly pleased to make their contribution,
Confident of its use, its rightfulness of place.

Pleased to demonstrate with calm gestures,
Flowing movements, these ancient rituals -
Combing, carding, spinning, weaving -
Talking easily the while of natural dyes,
Of sheep in pastures, grazing high or low,
The staple and the ply.

I listen, spell-bound, watch their placid hands,
Their unlined faces, smiling in repose;
These seem to summon me, appeal
To roots somewhere within my Self
Inviting me to stay, become
The person I am severed from.

WIVETON CHURCHYARD

Push open the iron kissing-gate
Turn, passing through,
To gain the churchyard,
See the view:
Across the gentle valley
Fields lie, tawny, ochre,
Yellow-green,
Divided by hedges,
Crowned by trees,

Bounded by a wall
Of brick and flint
Which ivies spill over
And hawthorns guard,
Stand monuments
Of local stone
In loving memory
Of people of the past;
Forever in the hearts
Of those who loved,
They're gone,
But not forgotten :

We're reminded
Not to weep
For those who
Rest in peace
Under the clear-washed skies,
Bird song, the soughing wind -
For who would fear to die
When this sweet continuity
With all they'd ever known
Could still be theirs?

FIRST TIME FOR SAMPHIRE

We've seen the boards:
 "Samphire For Sale"
Outside cottages
In several coastal hamlets
On our day trips, locally,
But never stopped to look -
Always on our way , I suppose,
To somewhere else.
I've remained curious
For a taste unknown -
Until this time ...

Self catering, today
I've nothing planned for tea.
We come to a village,
See the sign,
My husband volunteers, unusually,
"I'll get you some," he says;
Stops the car, and disappears
Behind the knapped-flint wall
Protecting the fishermen's dwellings
From the salty winds.

He's striding back now -
A latter-day hunter
Returning from the chase,
A paper-wrapped parcel
In his hands: it's huge!
"Here you are, then" he says triumphantly,
Slipping the package onto my lap.
"How much did you get?", I ask.
He starts the car.
"'Enough for four', I said :
That's what he gave me."

I'm doubtful still:
"It looks an awful lot",
Then, as we draw away:
"Did he say how to cook it?"
"Oh, I never thought to ask".

"Don't worry, Mum,
There's a recipe
On the souvenir tea-towel
That I've bought for Gran.
They call it 'poor man's asparagus',
You cook it much the same -
Serve it with melted butter.
It's very good, they say."

She's right -
And so are they!

A NORFOLK GATEWAY

High summer - and the heat
Has driven us out to seek
Some respite in the countryside.
Lanes shimmer as we go,
Car windows down,
Turning our faces to any breeze we find,
Grateful for passing shade of trees.

Panoramas lie all around us,
Colours paled by half-closed eyes,
When suddenly, around a curve
I see the gateway to a field of corn
With poppies, cornflowers,
Daisies by the post.

Instantly, I'm down the years
To when, a child, I stood amazed
At such a mix of colour -
Up to my waist and higher,
Noticing the spacing of the stems,
Drinking in the whispering
Of the close-packed ears;
Crouching to wonder
At the delicacy of petals,
Intimate insect markings
Seen from below.

I want so much a record of that time
Recaptured now on film:
I cry to stop, but these lanes are narrow
And we cannot park;
I'll walk back, then, to picture what I've seen -
But now there's no release
From high embankments,
And I must manage on my memories.

FEN FARM GEESE

There in the tussocky meadow's
Sea of green,
The deep-draft gander
And his mate
Walk Indian file.

On the narrow track
Which leads from the orchard
Through the half-closed gate,
They keep in perfect pace,
These two, coordinating contact
With low chuckling -
Their waggling tails
A private semaphore.

But , should you stray too near
The fence which borders
The pathway to the farmhouse door,
Cacophony breaks out ,
And you will be required
To explain to them, in full,
The reason for your presence here.

VIEW FROM A COTTAGE WINDOW

Beneath thatched eaves
The window, framed in white,
Gives onto coarse grasses,
Edging a stubbled field:
Just lately raked
By combine-harvester,
The corduroy lines scored there
Are feeding pheasants now.

Beyond that, and beyond again
I see another and
Another field -
Up to the horizon where
I know the lane to be
And little flint-walled,
Pantiled houses group.

Behind them flow
Parading clouds
Against the wide expanse
Of grey-blue sky.
Thirsty for beauty,
I drink in the view,
Hearing the cries of plovers,
Watching the slant
Of sudden autumn rain.

EVENING PLOUGHING

The dark earth furrows here
Are full of chipped flint -
Charcoal grey,
Oyster blue, amber,
Cream and dun .

Two blue Ford tractors
Towing devices for
The taming of the soil,
Toil along created lines,
Reach an end,
Lift their contraptions,
Turn, replace them,
And retrace.

The pungent smoke of fires
Drifts like mist
Across far fields,
Obscures the glimmer
Of the fading sun.

I watch, long minutes,
Till I feel
The chill of night set in,
Then turn,
Retrace,
Walk fast along the lane.

THETFORD STATION

Along the silent platform, half-barrels,
Red, pink-flowered, alternate,
Bask in the sharp light
Of September morning sun;
'Up' and 'Down' lines
Dance into distance
In the early heat.

In neat rows beyond the lineside fence,
Masses of dahlias -
Magenta, sulphur, crimson, pink -
As big as saucers, flame at the stake.
A hedge composed of runner beans in bloom
Forms the boundary of allotments there,
Small sheds, a pigeon loft ...

Beside enormous blue-green cabbages,
Emerald velvet cushions of parsley glow;
The yellow blossoms of potato plants
Shoot for the sky; currant bushes,
Heavy with ripe fruit,
Gleam red and black.

A few intending passengers
Tramp through
The echoing booking hall,
Over the footbridge,
Down the other side,
To stand about
Or sit on ornate benches
Whose cast iron logos: 'G.E.R.',
Proclaim past ownership.

A knot of parting friends
Carry on abstract conversation
Reduced to near-whispers
In the cathedral quiet.
There's a sudden squall of sound
As sparrows swoop under the canopy;
Fight it out in the gutterings,
As suddenly are gone.

Somewhere, a telegraph tings
Twice, peremptorily;
Rails sing.
A lone gardener, hoeing,
Eases his back to watch
A rattling two-car train arrive.
Its motors thrum, while passengers alight,
Others board.
Doors slam to farewell cries,
The motors rev, crescendo,
Change gear and leave behind
A shimmering haze of fumes,
As it pulls out.

The gardener resumes his work;
Only the clatter of the receding train
Borne on the settling air
Disturbs for moments longer
The station's quietude.

TIME OUT AT GLANDFORD

We've visited the Shell Museum,
Spent some time
Exclaiming quietly to one another
On the beauty , the sheer variety
Of the shells exhibited:

Infinitesimal, gigantic, they range
From ivory to deepest black,
Their iridescent linings
Rose-pink, flamingo red,
The silver-grey of pearl;
Corals of every hue.

Just now , we're sitting
In the nearby church.
Our eyes accustoming to the gloom,
We're appreciating peace
While the children go
To see the ducks
From the safety of the footbridge
Which spans the ford,
And marvel at the stillness
Of the mirroring pond
Which feeds the mill.

After a time,
We've finished looking round
At stained glass windows,
Depicting tranquil saints,
Bible scenes and personalities,
The Italian marble font,
And in the roof, carved angels,
On great hammer beams,
Of local cedar, oak.

Content, we're just about to leave
When, in the tower above our heads
Majestic rumblings occur,
Making us look at one another,
In surprise, and some alarm;

But then, the noise explains itself -
It's just the clock's workings
Making preparation to strike the hour;
It's three o'clock, and now,
We get, not just three chimes,
But a hymn tune played as well !

FAKENHAM MARKET DAY

First to the Auction -
Bidding starts eleven sharp,
Beginning outside
With hardware sundries.
Duck under the rope which marks
The boundary of the yard,
See, lined up for viewing,
Crates of tools;
Spades, forks and hoes
In heaps and bundles,
Tarpaulins, mowers and the like;
A wheelbarrow with assorted items,
A box of flowerpots, coils of hose;
Bicycles, all sizes, propped in a rack
Are causing interest to a knot of men
Who chuckle, reminiscing on their youth.

"Oh, look! an old iron mangle!"
A woman nudges her husband,
Points it out:
"My Nan had one of those."
They stand a moment in deference
To the memory, and then move on -
There's so much more to see ...

Men stand in well-knit groups,
In from the country for the day:
Flat caps, tweed hats,
Check shirts, cord trousers,
Quilted body-warmers,
Ex-Army pullovers,
Stout boots, high-polished shoes
Do sterling duty here.

The air is rich with local dialect;
Everyone seems to know everyone else -
No antagonisms here -
They're regulars, been coming here for years;
Laughter punctuates their every phrase,
Greets the end of every anecdote.
Their countenances show
Good-humoured lines, weathered
By sun, wind, rain - and life.
Some smoke, their cigarettes burn away
Between stubby, ingrained fingers,
Lips too busily employed to take a drag.

With thumbsticks in gnarled hands,
Their dogs on leads at heel,
Which sniff each others noses,
Gently waving tails,
They wait beside their chosen lots.

At last, the handbell's being rung
By an enthusiastic helper
Moving through the crowd: at once
A raised voice by Lot 1 begins
(There's no preamble here):
"Right! garden canes. Watmabid?"
(The tiniest pause)
'Tenner? Fiver? - Three, then?
One? and start !
One pound, one pound, two pounds,
Two pounds, two pounds, three,
Three pounds, at three then?"
(A sharp rap on his clip-board)
"Sold." A name is muttered,
Scribbled swiftly - on to the next:
"Two coils of heavy duty wire,
Petrol canister, sacks, never seen use ..."

POST CHRISTMAS BREAK - HUNSTANTON

'Just to the Lighthouse, then -
Let's stride it out !'

The cliff-top grass was white today -
Crunched deeply as we walked,
The wind keen, slicing at our ears.

Below the famed, striped cliffs,
The sand was rippled, static, crisp;
Salt sea heaved sluggishly
As, burdened with ice crystals
It shuffled to the shore
Like an oily slick,
Incredible to watch.

Gulls gleaned, stiff-legged,
Eyes half-closed,
Balls of wintery fluff,
Bunched indignantly
Against the bitter cold;
Yet they could have chosen
To take off into a cerulean sky,
Be nearer the brilliant sun
Which lit the town,
Showing the carr-stone buildings
To their best.

Refreshed by these contradictions
We've come in to eat,
Refuelling ourselves
To make our various journeys
Returning us to grey tarmac streets,
To concrete buildings
And the New Year's cares;
But as we sit at the table,
Wrapping our hands
Round mugs of warming soup,
We make Resolutions
To be here again, come Spring.